The AI Revolution: A Beginner's Guide to Practical Usage

AI SERIES _ 1

Erkan YILDIRIM

Table Of Contents

01

Chapter 1: Introduction to Artificial Intelligence

What is Artificial Intelligence?

Artificial Intelligence, or AI, is a term that is becoming increasingly familiar in our modern world. But what exactly is AI? In simple terms, AI refers to the development of computer systems that can perform tasks that typically require human intelligence. These tasks can range from recognizing speech and images to making decisions based on data analysis.

AI is a broad field that encompasses various subfields, including machine learning, neural networks, and natural language processing. Machine learning, in particular, is a key component of AI that involves teaching computers to learn from data without being explicitly programmed. This allows AI systems to improve their performance over time through experience.

The impact of AI is already being felt in our everyday lives, from personal assistants like Siri and Alexa to recommendation algorithms on streaming platforms like Netflix. But the potential applications of AI go far beyond consumer technology. In healthcare, AI is being used to analyze medical images and predict patient outcomes. In finance, AI is being used to detect fraud and optimize investment strategies.

Despite the exciting possibilities that AI presents, there are also concerns about its potential risks and ethical implications. Issues such as bias in AI algorithms, job displacement due to automation, and the potential for misuse of AI technology are all valid concerns that must be addressed as AI continues to advance.

Overall, AI is a powerful tool that has the potential to revolutionize industries and improve our daily lives. As we continue to explore the capabilities of AI, it is important to approach this technology with a critical eye and consider the ethical implications of its applications. By understanding what AI is and how it works, we can harness its potential for the greater good and navigate the challenges that come with it.

Brief History of AI

Artificial Intelligence, or AI, has become a hot topic in recent years, but its origins can be traced back to the 1950s. The term was first coined by computer scientist John McCarthy in 1956, and since then, AI has evolved significantly. Early AI systems were built to perform specific tasks, such as playing chess or solving mathematical problems, but as technology advanced, so did the capabilities of AI.

One of the key milestones in the history of AI was the development of expert systems in the 1970s. These systems were designed to mimic the decision-making processes of human experts in specific fields, such as medicine or finance. While expert systems were limited in their abilities, they laid the foundation for more advanced AI technologies to come. The 1980s and 1990s saw a surge in AI research and development, with the emergence of neural networks and machine learning algorithms. These technologies allowed AI systems to learn from data and improve their performance over time, leading to breakthroughs in speech recognition, image processing, and natural language processing.

In the early 2000s, AI began to be integrated into everyday products and services, such as virtual assistants, recommendation systems, and autonomous vehicles. These applications of AI have had a profound impact on our daily lives, making tasks easier and more efficient. As AI continues to advance, its potential for revolutionizing industries and shaping the future becomes more apparent.

Today, AI is being used in a wide range of industries, from healthcare and finance to marketing and manufacturing. The possibilities for AI are endless, and as the technology continues to evolve, it will be crucial for businesses and individuals to stay informed and adapt to the changing landscape. The history of AI is a testament to human ingenuity and innovation, and the future promises even greater advancements in this exciting field.

Types of AI Technologies

In the world of artificial intelligence (AI), there are various types of technologies that play a crucial role in shaping the landscape of the AI revolution. Understanding these different types of AI technologies is essential for anyone looking to harness the power of AI in their personal or professional lives. In this subchapter, we will explore some of the key types of AI technologies that are currently being utilized and developed.

One of the most common types of AI technologies is machine learning. Machine learning involves the use of algorithms and statistical models to enable computers to learn from and make predictions or decisions based on data. This type of AI technology is used in a wide range of applications, from recommendation systems to image recognition software. Machine learning is constantly evolving and improving, making it an exciting area of study for those interested in AI.

Another important type of AI technology is natural language processing (NLP). NLP is the ability of computers to understand, interpret, and generate human language. This technology is used in applications such as chatbots, virtual assistants, and language translation services. NLP is a rapidly growing field within AI, with many exciting developments on the horizon.

Computer vision is another type of AI technology that is gaining traction in various industries. Computer vision involves the use of algorithms to enable computers to interpret and understand visual information from the world around them. This technology is used in applications such as facial recognition, object detection, and autonomous vehicles. As computer vision technology continues to advance, we can expect to see even more innovative applications in the future.

Reinforcement learning is a type of AI technology that involves training a computer agent to make decisions based on rewards and feedback from its environment. This technology is used in applications such as game playing, robotics, and optimization problems. Reinforcement learning is a powerful tool for creating autonomous systems that can adapt and learn in real-time.

These are just a few examples of the types of AI technologies that are shaping the future of AI. As the field continues to evolve, we can expect to see even more exciting developments and applications in the years to come. Whether you are a curious newbie, a tech enthusiast, or a business-minded reader, understanding these different types of AI technologies is essential for staying informed and ahead of the curve in the AI revolution.

Importance of AI in Today's World

Artificial Intelligence (AI) has become an integral part of today's world, impacting various aspects of our daily lives. From enhancing customer experiences to revolutionizing industries, the importance of AI cannot be overlooked. In this subchapter, we will explore the significance of AI in today's world and how it is shaping our future.

One of the key reasons why AI is crucial in today's world is its ability to streamline processes and improve efficiency. AI-powered technologies can automate repetitive tasks, analyze large amounts of data, and make predictions based on patterns, ultimately saving time and resources for businesses and individuals alike. This efficiency boost has led to increased productivity and innovation across various industries.

Furthermore, AI plays a crucial role in enhancing customer experiences. From personalized recommendations on e-commerce platforms to chatbots providing instant customer support, AI technologies have transformed the way businesses interact with their customers. By leveraging AI, businesses can better understand their customers' needs and preferences, leading to improved satisfaction and loyalty.

In addition to improving efficiency and customer experiences, AI is also driving innovation and shaping the future of various industries. From healthcare to finance, AI-powered technologies are revolutionizing the way we approach challenges and come up with solutions. For example, AI is being used in healthcare to diagnose diseases, in finance to detect fraud, and in transportation to optimize routes, all with the aim of improving outcomes and efficiency.

Overall, the importance of AI in today's world cannot be understated. As AI continues to evolve and advance, it will play an increasingly vital role in shaping our future. Whether you are a curious newbie, a tech enthusiast, a business-minded reader, or a student looking to explore the world of AI, understanding the significance of AI in today's world is essential for staying informed and prepared for the AI revolution ahead.

02

Chapter 2: Practical Applications of AI in Everyday Life

AI in Personal Assistants

AI in personal assistants has revolutionized the way we interact with technology on a daily basis. From Siri to Alexa, these AI-powered assistants have become an integral part of our lives, helping us with tasks ranging from setting reminders to ordering groceries. The convenience and efficiency that these personal assistants offer have made them a popular choice for many individuals.

One of the key features of AI in personal assistants is their ability to learn and adapt to user preferences over time. Through machine learning algorithms, these assistants can analyze user behavior and tailor their responses accordingly. This personalized experience not only enhances user satisfaction but also improves the overall efficiency of the assistant.

Furthermore, AI in personal assistants has opened up new possibilities for multitasking and productivity. With the ability to perform multiple tasks simultaneously, these assistants can help users save time and stay organized. Whether it's scheduling meetings, sending emails, or providing real-time updates, AI-powered personal assistants can handle it all with ease.

Despite the numerous benefits of AI in personal assistants, there are also concerns surrounding privacy and security. As these assistants collect and store personal data, there is a risk of this information being compromised. It is essential for users to be aware of the potential risks and take necessary precautions to protect their privacy while using AI-powered personal assistants.

Overall, AI in personal assistants has significantly impacted our daily lives by providing convenience, efficiency, and personalized experiences. As this technology continues to evolve, it is important for users to stay informed about the latest developments and trends in order to make the most of their personal assistant experience. Whether you are a tech enthusiast, small business owner, or just curious about AI, personal assistants offer a glimpse into the future of AI for everyday life.

AI in Healthcare

Artificial Intelligence (AI) has made significant advancements in various industries, including healthcare. In recent years, AI technologies have been increasingly utilized to improve patient care, streamline administrative processes, and enhance medical research. This subchapter will explore the role of AI in healthcare and its potential impact on the industry.

One of the key areas where AI is being leveraged in healthcare is in diagnostics. AI algorithms have been developed to analyze medical imaging data, such as X-rays, MRIs, and CT scans, to assist healthcare professionals in detecting and diagnosing diseases. These AI systems can help radiologists and other specialists to identify abnormalities more accurately and efficiently, leading to earlier detection and treatment of medical conditions.

Another important application of AI in healthcare is personalized medicine. By analyzing large amounts of patient data, including genetic information, medical history, and lifestyle factors, AI can help healthcare providers to tailor treatment plans to individual patients. This approach can improve treatment outcomes and reduce the risk of adverse reactions to medications, ultimately leading to better patient care.

AI is also being used to improve operational efficiency in healthcare facilities. For example, AI-powered chatbots and virtual assistants can help patients schedule appointments, answer common medical questions, and provide personalized health advice. Additionally, AI algorithms can analyze patient data to predict hospital readmissions, optimize staffing levels, and streamline inventory management, leading to cost savings and improved patient outcomes.

While the potential benefits of AI in healthcare are significant, there are also challenges and concerns to consider. These include issues related to data privacy and security, ethical considerations surrounding the use of AI in making medical decisions, and the need for healthcare professionals to be trained in using AI technologies effectively. Despite these challenges, the integration of AI in healthcare has the potential to revolutionize the industry and improve patient care on a global scale.

AI in Education

Artificial Intelligence (AI) has the potential to revolutionize the field of education in numerous ways. From personalized learning experiences to improved administrative processes, AI has the power to enhance the way students learn and teachers teach. In this subchapter, we will explore the various applications of AI in education and discuss the potential impact it can have on the future of learning.

One of the key benefits of AI in education is its ability to personalize the learning experience for each student. By analyzing data on student performance and behavior, AI algorithms can tailor lessons to meet the individual needs and preferences of each student. This can help students learn at their own pace and in a way that is most effective for them, ultimately leading to improved academic outcomes.

AI can also assist teachers in various ways, such as automating administrative tasks, providing real-time feedback on student progress, and even creating personalized lesson plans. By freeing up teachers' time from routine tasks, AI allows them to focus on what they do best – teaching. This can lead to more engaged and motivated teachers, which in turn can have a positive impact on student learning.

Furthermore, AI can help identify students who may be struggling academically or emotionally, allowing educators to intervene early and provide the necessary support. By analyzing data on student behavior and performance, AI can detect patterns that may indicate a student is at risk and alert teachers and administrators. This proactive approach to student support can help prevent academic failure and improve overall student well-being.

In addition to personalized learning and teacher support, AI can also enhance the overall learning experience through immersive technologies such as virtual reality (VR) and augmented reality (AR). These technologies can create interactive and engaging learning environments that make learning more fun and effective. By incorporating AI-powered VR and AR tools into the classroom, educators can provide students with hands-on learning experiences that are both educational and entertaining.

Overall, the integration of AI in education has the potential to transform the way we teach and learn. From personalized learning experiences to improved teacher support and immersive technologies, AI has the power to revolutionize the field of education and create a more engaging and effective learning environment for students of all ages. As we continue to explore the possibilities of AI in education, we can look forward to a future where every student has the opportunity to reach their full potential.

AI has made significant strides in the entertainment industry, revolutionizing the way content is created, consumed, and personalized. From recommendation algorithms on streaming platforms to virtual reality experiences, AI is reshaping the entertainment landscape in exciting ways. This subchapter will explore the various applications of AI in entertainment and how it is transforming the industry.

AI in Entertainment

One of the most prominent uses of AI in entertainment is in content recommendation systems. Platforms like Netflix and Spotify use AI algorithms to analyze user preferences and behavior to suggest personalized content. These recommendation engines not only enhance user experience but also help companies increase user engagement and retention. By leveraging AI, entertainment companies can deliver tailored content to each user, leading to higher satisfaction and loyalty.

AI is also being used in the creation of content itself. For example, AI-powered tools can generate music, art, and even scripts for movies and TV shows. This technology enables creators to experiment with new ideas, styles, and formats, ultimately pushing the boundaries of traditional entertainment. Additionally, AI can be used to enhance special effects, animation, and post-production processes, making it easier and more cost-effective to produce high-quality content.

Virtual reality (VR) and augmented reality (AR) experiences are another area where AI is making a significant impact in entertainment. AI algorithms can enhance the realism and interactivity of VR/AR content by simulating realistic environments, characters, and interactions. This technology allows users to immerse themselves in virtual worlds and explore new forms of storytelling and entertainment. As VR and AR become more mainstream, AI will play a crucial role in shaping the future of entertainment.

In conclusion, AI is revolutionizing the entertainment industry by enabling personalized content recommendations, facilitating content creation, and enhancing VR/AR experiences. From music and movies to video games and live events, AI is transforming how we engage with and consume entertainment. As AI technology continues to evolve, we can expect to see even more innovative applications and experiences in the world of entertainment. Whether you are a content creator, consumer, or industry professional, understanding the role of AI in entertainment is essential for staying ahead of the curve in this rapidly evolving landscape.

AI in Transportation

AI in transportation is revolutionizing the way we move from one place to another, offering a glimpse into the future of smart and efficient transportation systems. From self-driving cars to traffic management, AI is playing a crucial role in making transportation safer, more convenient, and environmentally friendly.

One of the most prominent applications of AI in transportation is in the development of autonomous vehicles. These vehicles use AI algorithms to navigate roads, make decisions, and adapt to changing traffic conditions. Companies like Tesla, Waymo, and Uber are leading the way in developing self-driving cars that have the potential to reduce accidents, ease traffic congestion, and provide mobility solutions for those who are unable to drive.

AI is also being used to optimize traffic flow and reduce congestion in cities. By analyzing data from sensors, cameras, and GPS devices, AI systems can predict traffic patterns, identify bottlenecks, and recommend alternative routes in real-time. This not only saves time for commuters but also reduces fuel consumption and greenhouse gas emissions.

In addition to improving safety and efficiency, AI is also being used to enhance the overall passenger experience. For example, AI-powered chatbots and virtual assistants can provide real-time updates on travel conditions, recommend transportation options, and assist with booking tickets. This level of personalization and convenience is transforming the way we interact with transportation services.

As AI continues to advance, the transportation industry is poised to undergo a significant transformation. From self-driving cars to smart traffic management systems, AI has the potential to make transportation more accessible, sustainable, and enjoyable for people around the world. Whether you are a curious newbie, a tech enthusiast, or a business-minded reader, understanding the impact of AI in transportation is essential for navigating the future of transportation.

03

Chapter 3: Future Impact of AI on Society

Ethical Considerations of AI

In the world of artificial intelligence (AI), ethical considerations are paramount. As AI technology continues to advance at a rapid pace, it is crucial for users and developers to consider the ethical implications of their actions. From the potential for bias in algorithms to the impact on jobs and privacy, there are a myriad of ethical issues that must be taken into account.

One of the key ethical considerations of AI is the potential for bias in algorithms. AI systems are only as good as the data they are trained on, and if that data is biased, the results produced by the AI system will also be biased. This can have serious consequences, particularly in areas like hiring, lending, and criminal justice, where biased algorithms can perpetuate and even exacerbate existing inequalities.

Another ethical consideration of AI is the impact on jobs. As AI technology becomes more advanced, there is a concern that automation will lead to job loss in certain industries. While AI has the potential to create new jobs and increase productivity, it is important to consider the impact on workers who may be displaced by AI systems.

Privacy is also a significant ethical consideration when it comes to AI. As AI systems collect and analyze massive amounts of data, there is a risk that personal information could be misused or exploited. It is important for users and developers to prioritize data security and privacy protections to ensure that individuals' sensitive information is not compromised.

In addition to these ethical considerations, it is important to consider the broader societal impact of AI. From the potential for AI systems to exacerbate existing inequalities to the implications for democracy and human rights, there are a wide range of ethical issues that must be carefully considered. By approaching AI development and implementation with a strong ethical framework, we can ensure that AI technology is used responsibly and for the benefit of all.

Job Displacement and Automation

Job displacement and automation are two key topics in the realm of artificial intelligence that are causing both excitement and concern among various stakeholders. As AI technologies continue to advance at a rapid pace, many traditional job roles are at risk of being automated, leading to potential unemployment for millions of workers worldwide. This shift in the labor market is inevitable and poses challenges for individuals and organizations alike.

One of the main reasons for job displacement due to automation is the ability of AI systems to perform tasks more efficiently and accurately than humans. Tasks that are repetitive, predictable, and rule-based are particularly susceptible to automation, as AI algorithms can execute them with minimal error and at a fraction of the time it takes for a human to do the same task. This is evident in industries such as manufacturing, customer service, and transportation, where robots and AI-powered systems are increasingly taking over roles that were once performed by humans.

While the prospect of automation may seem daunting for workers whose jobs are at risk, it is important to acknowledge the potential benefits that AI can bring to the workforce. By automating routine tasks, employees can focus on more strategic, creative, and value-added activities that require human ingenuity and decision-making skills. This shift towards a more dynamic and skill-based workforce can lead to higher job satisfaction, increased productivity, and overall organizational growth.

For entrepreneurs and small business owners, the integration of AI technologies can offer significant competitive advantages in terms of cost savings, efficiency, and innovation. By leveraging AI-powered tools such as chatbots, predictive analytics, and robotic process automation, businesses can streamline operations, improve customer experiences, and stay ahead of the curve in a rapidly evolving market landscape. Embracing AI-driven automation can help smaller enterprises scale their operations, boost profitability, and drive sustainable growth in the long run.

In conclusion, job displacement and automation are inevitable consequences of the AI revolution, but they also present opportunities for individuals and organizations to adapt, innovate, and thrive in a technology-driven world. By understanding the impact of AI on the labor market and proactively preparing for the changes ahead, stakeholders can navigate the challenges and uncertainties of automation while harnessing the potential benefits of AI for everyday life. As we continue to explore the practical applications and future impact of AI, it is crucial for all stakeholders to stay informed, adaptable, and forward-thinking in order to leverage the power of artificial intelligence for positive outcomes.

AI in Government and Public Services

AI technology is increasingly being utilized in government and public services to improve efficiency, streamline processes, and enhance the overall quality of services provided to citizens. From predictive analytics to chatbots, AI is revolutionizing the way government agencies interact with the public and make decisions.

One of the key areas where AI is making a significant impact in government is in the realm of predictive analytics. By analyzing vast amounts of data, AI algorithms can help government agencies predict trends, anticipate needs, and make informed decisions. For example, AI can be used to predict traffic patterns, optimize public transportation routes, and even forecast demand for social services.

Another area where AI is being leveraged in government and public services is in the development of chatbots. These virtual assistants can help citizens navigate government websites, answer frequently asked questions, and provide real-time assistance. Chatbots are not only cost-effective but also provide a more efficient and personalized experience for citizens seeking information or services from government agencies.

AI is also being used to improve public safety and security. For example, AI-powered facial recognition technology can help law enforcement agencies identify suspects and prevent crime. Additionally, AI algorithms can analyze patterns in data to detect potential security threats and respond in real time to mitigate risks.

Overall, AI has the potential to transform government and public services in numerous ways, making them more efficient, responsive, and citizen-centric. However, there are also concerns about the ethical implications of AI in government, including issues related to privacy, transparency, and accountability. As AI continues to evolve and become more integrated into government operations, it will be crucial for policymakers, agencies, and citizens to work together to ensure that AI is used responsibly and ethically for the betterment of society.

AI in Environment and Sustainability

In recent years, artificial intelligence (AI) has been increasingly utilized in various fields, including environmental and sustainability efforts. From monitoring and managing natural resources to predicting climate change patterns, AI has proven to be a valuable tool in promoting a more sustainable future for our planet.

One of the key ways AI is being used in environmental initiatives is through data analysis and modeling. By processing large amounts of data collected from sensors, satellites, and other sources, AI algorithms can identify trends and patterns that humans may overlook. This information can then be used to make more informed decisions about resource management, conservation efforts, and pollution control.

AI is also being used to develop innovative solutions for environmental challenges. For example, AI-powered drones can be used to monitor wildlife populations, track deforestation, and assess the health of ecosystems. Similarly, AI algorithms can analyze weather data to predict natural disasters, such as hurricanes and wildfires, allowing for more effective emergency response and disaster preparedness.

In addition to monitoring and predicting environmental changes, AI can also help optimize resource usage and reduce waste. By analyzing data on energy consumption, water usage, and waste production, AI algorithms can identify inefficiencies and suggest ways to improve sustainability practices. This can lead to cost savings for businesses, as well as a reduced environmental impact.

Overall, the integration of AI in environmental and sustainability efforts offers great potential for addressing pressing global challenges. By harnessing the power of AI technology, we can work towards creating a more sustainable world for future generations. Whether you are a curious newcomer to AI, a tech enthusiast, or a business-minded entrepreneur, there are endless opportunities to explore and innovate in the realm of AI for environmental sustainability.

04

Chapter 4: Getting Started with AI

Understanding Machine Learning

Machine learning is a key concept in the field of artificial intelligence, and understanding it is crucial for anyone looking to harness the power of AI in their personal or professional lives. In simple terms, machine learning is a method of data analysis that allows computers to learn and improve from experience without being explicitly programmed. This process involves using algorithms to find patterns in data, which can then be used to make predictions or decisions.

For the curious newbie, machine learning may seem like a complex and intimidating topic, but it doesn't have to be. By breaking down the basic principles and applications of machine learning, even beginners can start to grasp the potential of this technology. From recommendation systems to image recognition, machine learning is already being used in a wide range of everyday applications, making our lives more convenient and efficient.

Tech enthusiasts and early adopters of technology are likely already familiar with the concept of machine learning, but may be interested in delving deeper into its inner workings. Understanding how machine learning algorithms work, and the different types of machine learning (such as supervised, unsupervised, and reinforcement learning), can provide valuable insights into how AI systems are trained and optimized.

Hobbyists and tinkerers may be interested in experimenting with machine learning themselves, using tools and platforms that make it easy to get started. Students and young professionals looking to enter the field of AI can benefit from gaining a solid understanding of machine learning, as it is a fundamental building block of many AI applications.

For the skeptical observer, understanding machine learning can help to demystify some of the hype surrounding AI and provide a more grounded perspective on its potential and limitations. By learning about the real-world applications of machine learning, skeptics may come to appreciate its practical benefits and contributions to society.

Whether you're a business-minded reader, an entrepreneur, a marketing professional, or a manager looking to stay ahead of the curve, understanding machine learning is essential for navigating the AI landscape. By recognizing the potential of machine learning to drive innovation and improve efficiency, you can position yourself and your organization to take advantage of the opportunities presented by AI for everyday life.

Tools and Resources for AI Beginners

Tools and resources for AI beginners are essential for those looking to dip their toes into the exciting world of artificial intelligence. Whether you are a curious newbie, a tech enthusiast, or an early adopter of technology, having the right tools at your disposal can make all the difference in your AI journey.

One of the most popular tools for AI beginners is Python, a versatile programming language that is commonly used in AI development. Python's simplicity and readability make it an ideal choice for those just starting out in AI. Additionally, there are a plethora of online resources and tutorials available for Python, making it easy to learn and experiment with AI projects.

Another valuable resource for AI beginners is TensorFlow, an open-source machine learning framework developed by Google. TensorFlow provides a wealth of tools and libraries for building and training AI models, making it an invaluable resource for those looking to delve deeper into the world of AI. With a vibrant online community and extensive documentation, TensorFlow is a great tool for AI beginners to explore.

For those interested in exploring the practical applications of AI in everyday life, platforms like IBM Watson and Microsoft Azure offer user-friendly tools and resources for developing AI projects. These platforms provide a range of services, from natural language processing to image recognition, allowing beginners to experiment with AI in a real-world context. Additionally, both IBM Watson and Microsoft Azure offer extensive documentation and support for beginners, making it easy to get started with AI projects.

In addition to tools and resources, AI beginners can also benefit from joining online communities and forums dedicated to artificial intelligence. Platforms like Reddit's r/artificial and Hacker News provide valuable insights, resources, and support for those looking to learn more about AI. By engaging with these communities, beginners can connect with like-minded individuals, ask questions, and stay up to date on the latest trends and developments in the world of AI. Overall, having the right tools and resources is essential for AI beginners to kickstart their journey into the exciting world of artificial intelligence.

Embarking on your first AI project can be an exciting and rewarding experience, especially in today's rapidly evolving technological landscape. Whether you are a curious newbie, a tech enthusiast, or an early adopter of technology, diving into the world of artificial intelligence opens up a world of possibilities. In this subchapter, we will guide you through the process of building your first AI project, from ideation to implementation.

The first step in building your AI project is to define a clear goal or problem that you want to solve. This could be anything from automating a repetitive task to predicting customer behavior. By clearly defining your objective, you will be able to focus your efforts and resources on developing a solution that meets your specific needs. Remember, the more specific and measurable your goal is, the easier it will be to track your progress and evaluate the success of your project.

Building Your First AI Project

Once you have defined your goal, the next step is to gather the necessary data. Data is the lifeblood of any AI project, as it is used to train machine learning models and make predictions. Depending on your project you may need to collect data from various sources, such as databases, APIs, or sensors. It is important to ensure that your data is accurate, relevant, and representative of the problem you are trying to solve. Additionally, you may need to preprocess and clean your data to remove any inconsistencies or errors that could affect the performance of your AI model.

With your data in hand, the next step is to choose the right tools and technologies for your AI project. There are a wide variety of AI frameworks, libraries, and platforms available that can help you build and deploy your AI models. Whether you are a hobbyist tinkering with AI for the first time or a student looking to gain practical experience, it is important to choose tools that are user friendly and well documented. Popular choices include TensorFlow, PyTorch, and scikit-learn, which offer a range of capabilities for building machine learning models.

Finally, once you have developed and tested your AI model, it is time to deploy it in a real-world setting. This could involve integrating your model into an existing application, building a custom interface for end users, or deploying it on a cloud platform for scalability. It is important to monitor the performance of your AI model in production and make any necessary adjustments to improve its accuracy and efficiency. By following these steps and staying curious and open-minded, you can successfully build your first AI project and unlock the potential of artificial intelligence in everyday life.

Joining the AI Community

Joining the AI community can be an exciting and rewarding experience for individuals from all walks of life. Whether you are a curious newbie, a tech enthusiast, an early adopter of technology, a hobbyist or tinkerer, a student or young professional, a skeptical observer, a business minded reader, an entrepreneur or small business owner, a marketing or sales professional, or a manager or leader, there is a place for you in the ever growing world of artificial intelligence.

One of the first steps to joining the AI community is to educate yourself on the basics of AI technology. This can be done through online courses, tutorials, workshops, and books like this one. By gaining a foundational understanding of AI concepts and terminology, you will be better equipped to engage with others in the community and contribute to discussions on the latest advancements in the field.

Another way to get involved in the AI community is to attend conferences, meetups, and networking events. These gatherings provide a valuable opportunity to connect with like minded individuals, learn from experts in the field, and discover new opportunities for collaboration and innovation. By actively participating in these events, you can expand your knowledge and network within the AI community.

For those interested in practical applications of AI for everyday life, there are countless opportunities to explore. From smart home devices and virtual assistants to autonomous vehicles and predictive analytics tools, AI technology is already shaping the way we live, work, and play. By experimenting with AI-powered tools and applications, you can gain hands-on experience and discover how this technology can enhance your daily routines and processes.

Ultimately, joining the AI community is about more than just learning about the latest trends and technologies – it is about becoming an active participant in shaping the future of AI. Whether you are a hobbyist tinkering with AI projects in your spare time or a business leader looking to leverage AI for strategic advantage, your contributions to the community are valuable and can help drive innovation and progress in this rapidly evolving field. So don't hesitate to jump in and join the AI community – the possibilities are endless!

05

Chapter 5: Overcoming Challenges and Pitfalls in AI

Bias and Fairness in AI

Bias and fairness in artificial intelligence (AI) are critically important topics that must be addressed as we continue to integrate AI into various aspects of our lives. While AI has the potential to revolutionize industries and improve efficiency, it is not without its flaws. Bias in AI systems can lead to unfair outcomes, perpetuate stereotypes, and even harm individuals or groups. It is essential for developers and users of AI technology to be aware of these issues and work towards creating more fair and unbiased AI systems.

One of the main reasons why bias can creep into AI systems is due to the data used to train these systems. If the data used is biased or incomplete, the AI system will learn from these biases and potentially perpetuate them in its decision-making processes. For example, if an AI system is trained on data that is skewed towards a certain demographic, it may make biased decisions that favor that demographic over others. This can lead to unfair outcomes for individuals who do not belong to the favored group.

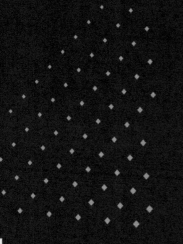

Another factor that can contribute to bias in AI systems is the algorithms used to process the data. If these algorithms are not designed with fairness in mind, they may inadvertently perpetuate biases that already exist in the data. For example, an algorithm that is trained to predict loan approval rates may inadvertently discriminate against certain groups based on factors such as race or gender if these biases are present in the training data. It is important for developers to carefully consider the potential biases in their algorithms and take steps to mitigate them.

To address bias and fairness in AI, it is crucial for developers to implement strategies to detect and mitigate bias in their systems. This can include conducting thorough audits of the training data to identify and remove biases, testing the algorithms for fairness using techniques such as fairness-aware machine learning, and incorporating diverse perspectives into the design and development process. By taking proactive steps to address bias, developers can create AI systems that are more fair and equitable for all users.

In conclusion, bias and fairness are important considerations in the development and deployment of AI systems. As AI technology continues to advance and become more integrated into our daily lives, it is crucial for developers, users, and policymakers to prioritize fairness and equity in AI systems. By being aware of the potential biases in AI systems, taking steps to mitigate them, and promoting diversity and inclusion in the development process, we can create AI systems that benefit society as a whole.

Data Privacy and Security Concerns

Data privacy and security concerns are paramount when it comes to the use of artificial intelligence (AI) in our everyday lives. As we entrust more and more of our personal information to AI systems, it is essential to understand the potential risks and take steps to protect ourselves. One of the biggest concerns surrounding AI is the collection and storage of vast amounts of personal data. AI systems rely on this data to learn and make decisions, but this raises questions about who has access to our information and how it is being used. It is important for users to be aware of the data being collected and to only share what is necessary for the AI system to function.

Another issue is the potential for data breaches and cyber attacks. AI systems are not immune to hacking, and a breach could result in the exposure of sensitive personal information. It is crucial for companies and developers to prioritize security measures when designing AI systems to prevent unauthorized access and protect user data.

Additionally, there is the concern of bias and discrimination in AI algorithms. If these systems are trained on biased data, they can perpetuate and even amplify existing prejudices. It is essential for developers to be mindful of the data they use to train AI models and to regularly audit their systems for bias.

In conclusion, while AI offers many benefits and opportunities for innovation, it is important to approach its use with caution and awareness of the potential privacy and security risks. By staying informed, practicing good data hygiene, and advocating for transparency and accountability in AI development, we can help ensure that these technologies are used responsibly and ethically.

Regulatory Compliance in AI

Regulatory compliance in AI is a crucial aspect that all individuals and businesses utilizing artificial intelligence technology must be aware of. As AI continues to revolutionize various industries and daily life, it is important to ensure that ethical and legal standards are being met. Regulatory compliance refers to the adherence to laws, regulations, and guidelines set forth by governing bodies to ensure that AI is being used responsibly and ethically.

One of the key reasons why regulatory compliance in AI is important is to protect the rights and privacy of individuals. With the vast amount of data being collected and analyzed by AI systems, there is a risk of this information being misused or exploited. Regulatory compliance helps to ensure that personal data is handled in a secure and ethical manner, protecting individuals from potential harm or discrimination.

Another important aspect of regulatory compliance in AI is to prevent bias and discrimination in decision-making processes. AI systems are only as good as the data they are trained on, and if this data is biased or flawed, it can lead to unfair outcomes. Regulatory compliance helps to ensure that AI systems are programmed and trained in a way that minimizes bias and discrimination, promoting fairness and equality in decision-making.

Additionally, regulatory compliance in AI helps to build trust and credibility with customers and stakeholders. By demonstrating a commitment to ethical and responsible AI practices, businesses can enhance their reputation and attract more customers. Compliance with regulations also helps to mitigate risks and avoid potential legal consequences, safeguardin g the interests of the business and its stakeholders.

In conclusion, regulatory compliance in AI is essential for ensuring that artificial intelligence is used in a responsible, ethical, and legal manner. By adhering to regulations and guidelines set forth by governing bodies, individuals and businesses can protect the rights and privacy of individuals, prevent bias and discrimination, and build trust and credibility with customers and stakeholders. Ultimately, regulatory compliance in AI is a key component of harnessing the full potential of artificial intelligence for the benefit of society.

Dealing with AI Failures and Mistakes

In the fast-paced world of artificial intelligence (AI), failures and mistakes are inevitable. As we rely more and more on AI technology in our everyday lives, it is crucial to understand how to handle these failures effectively. In this subchapter, we will explore some common reasons for AI failures and mistakes, as well as strategies for dealing with them.

One of the main reasons for AI failures is a lack of data. AI algorithms rely on large amounts of data to make accurate predictions and decisions. If the data used to train the AI model is biased, incomplete, or outdated, it can result in errors and mistakes. To mitigate this risk, it is essential to regularly review and update the data used in AI systems.

Another common cause of AI failures is poor algorithm design. AI algorithms are complex and can be prone to bugs and errors. It is crucial to thoroughly test and validate AI models before deploying them in real world applications. Additionally, ongoing monitoring and evaluation of AI systems can help identify and address any issues that arise.

When AI failures occur, it is important to have a plan in place to address them quickly and effectively. This may involve retraining the AI model with new data, adjusting the algorithm parameters, or even redesigning the entire AI system. It is also essential to communicate transparently with users and stakeholders about the nature of the failure and the steps being taken to address it.

Ultimately, dealing with AI failures and mistakes requires a combination of technical expertise, critical thinking, and effective communication. By understanding the common reasons for AI failures and implementing strategies to address them, we can harness the power of AI technology while minimizing the risks. As AI continues to revolutionize our world, being prepared to handle failures and mistakes will be essential for success in the AI driven future.

Chapter 6: AI and Business

AI for Marketing and Sales

In today's rapidly evolving digital landscape, artificial intelligence (AI) has become a powerful tool for marketing and sales professionals. AI technology has the ability to analyze vast amounts of data in real-time, providing valuable insights into consumer behavior and preferences. This enables businesses to create more targeted and personalized marketing campaigns, leading to increased customer engagement and sales.

One of the key benefits of using AI for marketing and sales is its ability to automate repetitive tasks, such as data analysis and lead generation. This allows marketing teams to focus on more strategic initiatives, while AI takes care of the routine tasks. By leveraging AI-powered tools, businesses can streamline their marketing and sales processes, saving time and resources in the long run.

AI also has the potential to revolutionize the way businesses interact with their customers. Chatbots, for example, can provide instant customer support and assistance, improving the overall customer experience. AI algorithms can also analyze customer feedback and sentiment, helping businesses to better understand their target audience and tailor their marketing strategies accordingly.

For entrepreneurs and small business owners, AI can level the playing field by providing access to sophisticated marketing and sales tools that were once only available to larger corporations. By harnessing the power of AI, small businesses can compete more effectively in the marketplace, reaching new customers and driving growth.

Overall, AI for marketing and sales is a game-changer for businesses of all sizes. By embracing AI technology, marketing and sales professionals can gain a competitive edge, improve customer relationships, and drive business growth. As AI continues to advance, we can expect to see even more innovative applications in the world of marketing and sales, making it an exciting time to be at the forefront of this AI revolution.

AI for Customer Service

In the ever-evolving landscape of customer service, artificial intelligence (AI) is becoming increasingly prevalent. AI for customer service offers a wide range of benefits, from improving efficiency and reducing costs to enhancing customer satisfaction. In this subchapter, we will explore the ways in which AI is revolutionizing the customer service industry and how businesses can leverage this technology to their advantage.

One of the key advantages of using AI for customer service is its ability to handle a high volume of inquiries quickly and efficiently. AI-powered chatbots, for example, can provide instant responses to customer queries, freeing up human agents to focus on more complex issues. This not only improves response times but also ensures that customers receive timely assistance, leading to higher levels of satisfaction.

Furthermore, AI can help businesses gain valuable insights into customer behavior and preferences. By analyzing data from customer interactions, AI can identify patterns and trends that can be used to personalize the customer experience. For example, AI can recommend products or services based on a customer's browsing history or past purchases, making it easier for businesses to upsell and cross-sell to their customers.

AI for customer service also has the potential to reduce costs for businesses. By automating routine tasks such as answering basic inquiries or processing returns, businesses can save time and resources. This not only increases efficiency but also allows businesses to reallocate their human resources to more strategic tasks, ultimately driving growth and innovation.

Despite the many benefits of AI for customer service, some may be skeptical of its effectiveness. However, studies have shown that AI-powered customer service solutions can lead to higher customer satisfaction rates and improved customer loyalty. By embracing AI, businesses can stay ahead of the curve and deliver a superior customer experience that sets them apart from the competition.

In conclusion, AI for customer service is a game-changer for businesses looking to streamline their operations, improve customer satisfaction, and drive growth. By leveraging AI-powered solutions, businesses can gain a competitive edge in today's fast-paced digital world. Whether you are a curious newbie, a tech enthusiast, or a business-minded reader, understanding the potential of AI for customer service is essential for staying ahead of the curve in the AI revolution.

AI for Operations and Efficiency

In today's fast-paced world, the use of Artificial Intelligence (AI) has become increasingly prevalent in various industries. From healthcare to finance, AI is revolutionizing the way businesses operate and helping them achieve greater efficiency. In this subchapter, we will explore the role of AI in operations and efficiency, and how it can benefit individuals and businesses alike.

One of the key areas where AI is making a significant impact is in operations management. AI-powered systems can analyze vast amounts of data in real-time, allowing businesses to make informed decisions quickly and efficiently. For example, AI algorithms can optimize supply chain management by predicting demand, reducing inventory costs, and improving delivery times. This not only saves time and money but also enhances overall operational efficiency.

Furthermore, AI can automate repetitive tasks, freeing up employees to focus on more strategic and creative endeavors. For instance, chatbots powered by AI can handle customer inquiries, reducing the workload on customer service representatives. This not only improves customer satisfaction but also allows businesses to operate more efficiently by streamlining their operations. In addition to improving operations, AI can also enhance efficiency in various aspects of business, such as marketing and sales. AI-powered tools can analyze consumer behavior patterns, predict trends, and personalize marketing campaigns to target specific audiences effectively. This targeted approach not only increases conversion rates but also reduces marketing costs and improves overall efficiency in driving sales.

For entrepreneurs and small business owners, AI offers a wealth of opportunities to streamline their operations and improve efficiency. Whether it's automating administrative tasks, optimizing inventory management, or enhancing customer service, AI can help small businesses operate more effectively and compete with larger enterprises. By embracing AI technologies, entrepreneurs can gain a competitive edge and drive growth in their businesses.

Overall, AI for operations and efficiency is not just a trend but a necessity in today's digital age. By harnessing the power of AI, individuals and businesses can optimize their operations, improve efficiency, and stay ahead of the curve in a rapidly evolving marketplace. Whether you're a tech enthusiast, a business-minded reader, or a curious newbie, exploring the possibilities of AI in operations and efficiency can open up a world of opportunities for innovation and growth.

AI for Strategic Decision Making

In the world of business, making strategic decisions is crucial for success. With the rapid advancements in artificial intelligence (AI) technology, businesses now have a powerful tool at their disposal to aid in this process. AI can analyze vast amounts of data, identify patterns, and provide valuable insights that can inform strategic decision making.

One key benefit of using AI for strategic decision making is its ability to process and analyze data at a speed and scale that far exceeds human capabilities. This means that businesses can quickly gather and assess information from a variety of sources to make more informed decisions. By leveraging AI, businesses can gain a competitive edge by making decisions based on data-driven insights rather than gut feelings or intuition.

AI can also help businesses identify trends and opportunities that may not be immediately apparent to human decision makers. By analyzing data from multiple sources, AI can uncover correlations and patterns that can help businesses anticipate market shifts, identify emerging trends, and make proactive decisions to stay ahead of the competition.

Furthermore, AI can assist in scenario planning and risk analysis, allowing businesses to assess the potential outcomes of different strategic decisions before they are implemented. By simulating various scenarios and assessing their potential impact, businesses can make more informed decisions that are based on a comprehensive understanding of the potential risks and rewards.

Overall, AI has the potential to revolutionize strategic decision making in business by providing valuable insights, identifying opportunities, and helping businesses anticipate and mitigate risks. As AI technology continues to evolve and improve, businesses that harness its power for strategic decision making will be better equipped to navigate the complexities of the modern business landscape and achieve sustainable success.

07

Chapter 7: The Future of AI

Advancements in AI Technology

Advancements in AI technology have been rapidly evolving in recent years, revolutionizing the way we interact with machines and enhancing our daily lives in ways we never thought possible. From virtual assistants like Siri and Alexa to self driving cars and personalized recommendations on streaming platforms, artificial intelligence is becoming increasingly integrated into our everyday activities.

One of the most significant advancements in AI technology is the development of machine learning algorithms. These algorithms allow computers to learn from data and make decisions without being explicitly programmed to do so. This has led to breakthroughs in areas such as natural language processing, image recognition, and predictive analytics, enabling AI systems to perform complex tasks with remarkable accuracy.

Another exciting advancement in AI technology is the rise of deep learning networks. These neural networks are inspired by the structure of the human brain and are capable of processing vast amounts of data to recognize patterns and make predictions. Deep learning has been instrumental in powering advancements in speech recognition, autonomous vehicles, and facial recognition technology.

AI technology has also made significant strides in the healthcare industry, with the development of medical imaging tools that can detect diseases like cancer at an early stage. AI-powered robots are also being used in surgery to assist doctors and improve patient outcomes. These advancements have the potential to revolutionize the way we approach healthcare and save lives.

Overall, the advancements in AI technology are reshaping our world in profound ways, from improving our daily routines to transforming industries like healthcare, finance, and transportation. As AI continues to evolve, it is crucial for individuals and businesses to stay informed and adapt to these changes to harness the full potential of artificial intelligence. Whether you are a curious newbie, a tech enthusiast, or a business-minded professional, understanding the advancements in AI technology is essential for navigating the future of technology and unlocking new opportunities for growth and innovation.

AI in Robotics and Automation

Artificial Intelligence (AI) has revolutionized the field of robotics and automation, paving the way for incredible advancements in various industries. From manufacturing to healthcare, AI-powered robots are transforming the way tasks are performed, increasing efficiency, productivity, and accuracy. In this subchapter, we will delve into the role of AI in robotics and automation, exploring the potential benefits and challenges that come with this cutting-edge technology.

One of the key advantages of integrating AI into robotics and automation is the ability to perform complex tasks with precision and speed. AI algorithms allow robots to analyze data in real-time, making decisions and adjustments on the fly to optimize performance. This level of intelligence enables robots to adapt to changing environments and interact with humans in a more natural and intuitive way. As a result, companies can streamline their operations, reduce costs, and improve overall quality and consistency.

Furthermore, AI-powered robots are revolutionizing industries that require repetitive and labor-intensive tasks, such as manufacturing and logistics. By automating these processes, companies can increase production capacity, reduce human error, and improve workplace safety. Additionally, AI can enhance the capabilities of robots by enabling them to learn from experience and continuously improve their performance over time. This self-learning aspect of AI is revolutionizing the concept of robotics, paving the way for more autonomous and intelligent machines.

However, the integration of AI in robotics and automation also presents challenges and concerns that must be addressed. One of the main concerns is the potential impact on the workforce, as automation may lead to job displacement in certain industries. It is essential for companies to consider the ethical implications of AI deployment and ensure that appropriate measures are taken to support and retrain employees affected by automation. Additionally, there are concerns about the reliability and safety of AI-powered robots, as errors or malfunctions could have serious consequences in critical applications. Despite these challenges, the future of AI in robotics and automation is bright, with endless possibilities for innovation and advancement. As AI technology continues to evolve, we can expect to see even more sophisticated robots capable of performing a wide range of tasks with precision and efficiency. For businesses, embracing AI in robotics and automation can lead to increased competitiveness, improved customer satisfaction, and new opportunities for growth and expansion. As we navigate this AI revolution, it is crucial for individuals and organizations to stay informed, adapt to new technologies, and seize the opportunities that AI presents for a brighter and more efficient future.

AI in Space Exploration

In recent years, artificial intelligence (AI) has revolutionized many industries, including space exploration. AI is playing a crucial role in helping scientists and engineers explore the vast unknowns of space more efficiently and effectively. From autonomous rovers on Mars to predictive analytics for satellite communication, AI is transforming the way we study and understand our universe.

One of the key areas where AI is making a significant impact in space exploration is in autonomous robots and rovers. These intelligent machines are able to navigate harsh terrain, collect data, and make decisions without human intervention. For example, NASA's Mars rovers, such as Curiosity and Perseverance, use AI algorithms to analyze images, identify interesting rocks, and plan their own routes. This autonomy allows these robots to explore more efficiently and cover more ground than if they were controlled remotely by humans.

Another important application of AI in space exploration is in predictive analytics for satellite communication. AI algorithms can analyze massive amounts of data from satellites in real-time to predict potential failures or anomalies. By detecting issues before they occur, engineers can take preventative measures to ensure the smooth operation of communication satellites, which are vital for relaying data and images back to Earth from spacecraft and rovers.

Furthermore, AI is also being used in space exploration to optimize mission planning and resource allocation. By analyzing vast amounts of data, AI algorithms can recommend the most efficient routes for spacecraft, minimize fuel consumption, and allocate resources effectively. This not only saves time and money but also increases the chances of successful missions by ensuring that resources are used wisely.

Overall, AI is revolutionizing the field of space exploration by enabling scientists and engineers to explore the cosmos more efficiently and effectively. From autonomous robots on Mars to predictive analytics for satellite communication, AI is helping us push the boundaries of what is possible in our quest to understand the universe. As AI technology continues to advance, we can expect even more exciting developments in space exploration in the years to come.

Ethical AI Development and Governance

In the rapidly evolving landscape of artificial intelligence (AI), the importance of ethical AI development and governance cannot be overstated. As we witness the incredible advancements in AI technology, it is crucial to consider the ethical implications of these innovations. Ethical AI development involves ensuring that AI systems are designed and implemented in a way that upholds values such as fairness, transparency, accountability, and privacy.

One of the key principles of ethical AI development is fairness. It is essential to ensure that AI systems do not perpetuate biases or discriminate against certain groups of people. This requires careful consideration of the data used to train AI models, as well as the algorithms and decision-making processes employed. By prioritizing fairness in AI development, we can create systems that benefit all members of society equitably.

Transparency is another critical aspect of ethical AI development. Users should have a clear understanding of how AI systems make decisions and why they produce certain outcomes. This transparency not only builds trust with users but also allows for greater accountability in the event of errors or unintended consequences. By promoting transparency in AI development, we can foster a culture of openness and accountability in the AI industry.

Accountability is also a vital component of ethical AI development and governance. Developers and organizations must take responsibility for the impact of their AI systems on individuals, communities, and society as a whole. This includes addressing any harm caused by AI systems and taking steps to mitigate risks and ensure compliance with regulatory standards. By holding developers and organizations accountable for their AI systems, we can promote responsible innovation and protect the interests of all stakeholders.

Privacy is another key consideration in ethical AI development. As AI systems collect and analyze vast amounts of data, it is essential to safeguard individuals' privacy rights and ensure that data is used in a responsible and ethical manner. By prioritizing privacy in AI development, we can build trust with users and ensure that AI systems respect and protect individuals' personal information. Ultimately, by incorporating ethical principles such as fairness, transparency, accountability, and privacy into AI development and governance, we can create AI systems that benefit society while upholding ethical standards and values.

08

Chapter 8:
Conclusion

Summary of Key Points

In this subchapter, we will summarize the key points discussed throughout the book "The AI Revolution: A Beginner's Guide to Practical Usage." For the curious newbie, tech enthusiast, early adopters, hobbyists, students, and young professionals, this book serves as a comprehensive introduction to the world of artificial intelligence and its practical applications. First and foremost, we have explored the various ways in which AI is already impacting our everyday lives. From virtual assistants like Siri and Alexa to recommendation algorithms on streaming platforms, AI is all around us and is becoming increasingly integrated into our daily routines. It is important for individuals in all niches to understand how AI works and how it can be leveraged for personal and professional growth.

For the skeptical observer, this book provides a balanced view of the potential benefits and challenges of AI. While AI has the power to revolutionize industries and improve efficiency, there are also concerns about job displacement and ethical implications. It is crucial to approach AI with a critical mindset and to be aware of both its strengths and limitations.

For the business-minded reader, entrepreneurs, small business owners, marketing and sales professionals, managers, and leaders, this book offers insights into how AI can be used to drive growth and innovation within organizations. From automating routine tasks to analyzing customer data for personalized marketing campaigns, AI has the potential to transform the way businesses operate and interact with their customers.

In conclusion, "The AI Revolution" serves as a valuable resource for individuals interested in understanding the practical applications and future impact of AI. Whether you are a curious newcomer to the world of AI or a seasoned professional looking to stay ahead of the curve, this book provides a comprehensive overview of the opportunities and challenges presented by this rapidly evolving technology. It is essential for all readers to stay informed and engaged with the advancements in AI in order to navigate the changing landscape of our digital world.

Final Thoughts on the AI Revolution

As we come to the end of this journey through the AI revolution, it is important to reflect on the impact that artificial intelligence has had on our everyday lives. For the curious newbie, the tech enthusiast, and early adopters of technology, AI has opened up a world of possibilities, from personalized recommendations to smart home devices that make our lives easier and more efficient. For hobbyists and tinkerers, the possibilities for using AI in DIY projects are endless. Whether it's creating a voice-controlled robot or using machine learning algorithms to analyze data, AI provides a new avenue for exploration and innovation. Students and young professionals have a unique opportunity to learn and develop their skills in AI, as the demand for AI expertise continues to grow in the job market.

For the skeptical observer, it is important to acknowledge both the potential benefits and risks of AI. While AI has the potential to revolutionize industries and improve our quality of life, there are also concerns about privacy, bias, and job displacement. It is crucial that we approach the development and deployment of AI technologies with caution and ethical considerations in mind.

For the business-minded reader, entrepreneurs, and small business owners, AI presents a wealth of opportunities for growth and innovation. From optimizing processes to improving customer experiences, AI can help businesses stay competitive in a rapidly changing landscape. Marketing and sales professionals can leverage AI tools to better understand their customers and target their messaging effectively.

For managers and leaders, it is important to embrace AI as a tool for driving innovation and growth within their organizations. By investing in AI technologies and fostering a culture of experimentation and learning, businesses can stay ahead of the curve and adapt to the changing demands of the market. The AI revolution is here to stay, and it is up to all of us to harness its potential for the betterment of society and the advancement of technology.

Resources for Further Learning and Exploration

In the rapidly evolving world of artificial intelligence, there are countless resources available for those looking to deepen their understanding and explore the possibilities of this groundbreaking technology. Whether you are a curious newbie, a tech enthusiast, an early adopter, a hobbyist, a student, a young professional, a skeptical observer, a business-minded individual, an entrepreneur, a marketing professional, a manager, or a leader, there are resources tailored to your specific interests and needs.

For those just beginning their journey into the world of AI, online courses and tutorials can provide a solid foundation of knowledge. Websites like Coursera, Udemy, and Khan Academy offer a wide range of courses on topics such as machine learning, neural networks, and natural language processing. These courses are designed to be accessible to beginners while still providing valuable insights and practical skills.

For those looking to stay up-to-date on the latest developments in AI, podcasts and blogs can be a valuable resource. Podcasts like "The AI Podcast" by NVIDIA and "This Week in Machine Learning & AI" provide in-depth discussions on current trends and breakthroughs in the field. Similarly, blogs like Towards Data Science and AI Trends offer insightful articles and analysis on a wide range of AI-related topics.

Books are another valuable resource for those looking to deepen their understanding of AI. Titles like "Artificial Intelligence: A Guide for Thinking Humans" by Melanie Mitchell and "Superintelligence: Paths, Dangers, Strategies" by Nick Bostrom offer comprehensive overviews of the field and explore the potential impact of AI on society. These books are perfect for those looking for a more in-depth exploration of AI and its implications. For those interested in hands-on experience with AI, online coding platforms like Kaggle and GitHub offer opportunities to work on real-world AI projects and collaborate with other enthusiasts. These platforms provide a valuable opportunity to apply theoretical knowledge to practical applications and develop valuable skills that can be applied in a professional setting.

In conclusion, the world of artificial intelligence is vast and complex, but with the right resources and tools, anyone can begin to explore its potential and make meaningful contributions to the field. Whether you are a beginner looking to learn the basics or a seasoned professional seeking to stay ahead of the curve, there are resources available to help you on your journey into the exciting world of AI.

AI Made Simple
Your Guide to the Future You Didn't Know Existed

Ever wonder how your phone "knows" what you're about to type or how your music streaming service suggests songs you love? That's the power of Artificial Intelligence (AI)! This book is your friendly guide to understanding this fascinating technology and how it's already changing your world (and will keep on changing it!). **Inside, you'll discover:** * **Simple explanations of AI concepts:** No confusing jargon here! We'll break down AI in terms you can understand. * **Real-world examples:** See how AI is impacting everything from your daily commute to your healthcare. * **The future of AI:** Explore the exciting possibilities of AI-powered homes, transportation, and even education! **Whether you're a young adult navigating a changing job market, a parent curious about your child's future, or a senior interested in smart home technology, this book will help you embrace the future with confidence.** **Embrace the Future of AI Today!**